Early civilizations of the
Americas

EARLY CIVILIZATIONS OF THE
AMERICAS

ANCIENT CIVILIZATIONS

EARLY CIVILIZATIONS OF THE
AMERICAS

Edited by Michael Anderson

Britannica
Educational Publishing
IN ASSOCIATION WITH

ROSEN
EDUCATIONAL SERVICES

Published in 2012 by Britannica Educational Publishing
(a trademark of Encyclopædia Britannica, Inc.)
in association with Rosen Educational Services, LLC
29 East 21st Street, New York, NY 10010.

Distributed exclusively by Rosen Educational Services.
For a listing of additional Britannica Educational Publishing titles, call toll free (800) 237-9932.

First Edition

Britannica Educational Publishing
Michael I. Levy: Executive Editor, Encyclopædia Britannica
J.E. Luebering: Director, Core Reference Group, Encyclopædia Britannica
Adam Augustyn: Assistant Manager, Encyclopædia Britannica

Anthony L. Green: Editor, Compton's by Britannica
Michael Anderson: Senior Editor, Compton's by Britannica
Sherman Hollar: Associate Editor, Compton's by Britannica

Marilyn L. Barton: Senior Coordinator, Production Control
Steven Bosco: Director, Editorial Technologies
Lisa S. Braucher: Senior Producer and Data Editor
Yvette Charboneau: Senior Copy Editor
Kathy Nakamura: Manager, Media Acquisition

Rosen Educational Services
Heather M. Moore Niver: Editor
Nelson Sá: Art Director
Cindy Reiman: Photography Manager
Karen Huang: Photo Researcher
Matthew Cauli: Designer, Cover Design
Introduction by Michael Anderson and Heather M. Moore Niver

Library of Congress Cataloging-in-Publication Data

Early civilizations of the Americas / edited by Michael Anderson.
   p. cm. — (Ancient civilizations)
"In association with Britannica Educational Publishing, Rosen Educational Services."
Includes bibliographical references and index.
ISBN 978-1-61530-525-4 (library binding)
1. Indians—History—Juvenile literature. 2. Indians—Social life and customs—Juvenile literature. 3.
America—Antiquities—Juvenile literature. I. Anderson, Michael, 1972-
E58.4.E24 2012
970.01—dc22

                                                                                    2011006335

Manufactured in the United States of America

On the cover, page 3: Pyramid of the Sun, Teotihuacán, Mexico. *Shutterstock.com*

Pages 10, 21, 47, 60, 78, © www.istockphoto.com/Darla Hallmark; pp. 12, 20, 40,
58, 64, 65 © www.istockphoto.com/Darek Niedzieski; remaining interior background image
© www.istockphoto.com/David Pedre; back cover Shutterstock.com

70.01
2a

CONTENTS

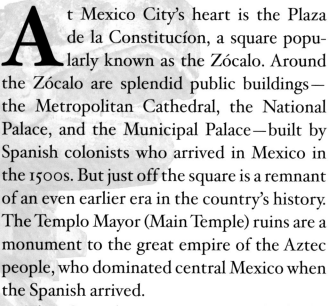

At Mexico City's heart is the Plaza de la Constitucíon, a square popularly known as the Zócalo. Around the Zócalo are splendid public buildings—the Metropolitan Cathedral, the National Palace, and the Municipal Palace—built by Spanish colonists who arrived in Mexico in the 1500s. But just off the square is a remnant of an even earlier era in the country's history. The Templo Mayor (Main Temple) ruins are a monument to the great empire of the Aztec people, who dominated central Mexico when the Spanish arrived.

The Spanish conquerors methodically destroyed the Aztec capital, Tenochtitlán, and constructed Mexico City over the rubble of its temples and palaces. They could not, however, erase the memory of the civilization they displaced. This book examines the Aztec Empire and other advanced Indian civilizations of the ancient Americas. Among them are the Maya and the Inca, which rank alongside the Aztec as the best-known ancient civilizations. But also here are many lesser-known cultures that are remarkable for their own achievements, whether in agriculture, social organization, architecture, the arts, or other areas.

The earliest Americans were the Paleo-Indians, who migrated from Asia during the last ice age. Nomadic hunters and gatherers, they relied on big game like mammoths as well as wild plant foods. Eventually, environmental changes such as dramatically increasing temperatures caused the largest animals to die off, so Indians turned to alternatives like elk and fish. They also remained in one area for longer periods and began farming. These changes are characteristic of the Archaic Indian cultures.

The greatest agricultural advancements of the Archaic period occurred in Middle and South America. Having domesticated crops like corn and squash as early as 8000 BC, Middle American Indians could

The ruins of the Incan city of Machu Picchu still stand in south-central Peru. Shutterstock.com

settle into villages and focus on arts and commerce. By about 1200 BC, the first elaborate Indian civilization in the region, that of the Olmec, had appeared. The Olmec built large towns and created extraordinary stonework, including their renowned "colossal heads."

Later Indian cultures in Middle America showed the influence of the Olmec. In the first millennium AD these civilizations created the first cities in the Western Hemisphere. The Maya of Guatemala and the Yucatán Peninsula built cities with stone temples, pyramids, palaces, ball courts, and plazas. They also reached great heights in astronomy, mathematics, calendar making, and hieroglyphic writing. During the same period, Teotihuacán, near present-day Mexico City, housed some 150,000 people, making it one of the largest cities in the world. Later came the Toltec and then the Aztec.

In South America's Andes Mountains, complex civilizations began to develop in about 2300 BC. The earliest Andean civilizations include the Tiwanaku and Chimú kingdoms, which occupied lands in Bolivia and Peru. When the Spanish came to Peru in 1532, the Inca controlled an extensive empire. The Machu Picchu ruins reveal outstanding architecture and stepped agricultural fields

watered by long aqueducts. The Inca had a highly stratified social hierarchy led by their emperor, who was considered a child of the Sun and ruled by divine right.

The Indians of Northern America (present-day United States and Canada) developed farming villages a little later than the peoples of Middle and South America. In the Southwest, the Ancestral Pueblo, Mogollon, and Hohokam managed to grow corn, squash, and other crops by using irrigation to overcome the dry climate. In the East, the most extensive prehistoric farming culture was created by the Mississippian Indians. Mississippian towns, characterized by huge earthen mounds topped by temples, were scattered throughout the Southeast and the Northeast.

Through the years, many accounts of American history have begun with the arrival of European explorers and colonists in the New World. As this book amply illustrates, however, the story of the Americas started long before the first European ships landed on their shores. Read on to meet the Maya, Aztec, Inca, and other remarkable ancient Americans.

CHAPTER 1
THE ORIGINS OF EARLY AMERICAN CIVILIZATIONS

The first people to live in the Americas were the Indians, or Native Americans. Their settlements ranged across the Western Hemisphere and were built on many of the sites where modern cities now rise. Indian families and traders used paths now followed by roads and railroads. Indian farmers were the first in the world to domesticate corn (maize), beans, squash, potatoes, tomatoes, and many other food plants that help feed the peoples of the world today. These resources, along with others provided by hunting, gathering, and fishing, were used to support communities ranging from small villages to expansive cities with tens of thousands of residents.

The first Indians arrived during the last ice age, when thick ice sheets covered much of northern North America. As the ice sheets absorbed water, sea levels dropped and a land bridge emerged along the present-day Bering Strait. From about 30,000 to 12,000 years ago the land bridge connected

Early humans crossed from northeastern Asia to the Americas over a now-submerged land bridge across the Bering Strait. The locations of archaeological sites in the Americas suggest the migration routes followed by Paleo-Indians after the glaciers of the late Pleistocene Epoch melted.

northeastern Asia to what is now Alaska. Humans began to cross over from Asia at least 13,000 years ago and perhaps much earlier. When the ice sheets melted, the land bridge disappeared under the rising seas and the migration ended.

THE CLOVIS AND FOLSOM DISCOVERIES

In 1908 George McJunkin, a ranch foreman and former slave, reported that the bones of an extinct form of giant bison were eroding out of a wash near Folsom, N.M. An ancient spear point was later found embedded in the animal's skeleton. In 1929 teenager Ridgley Whiteman found a similar site near Clovis, N.M., albeit with mammoth rather than bison remains. The Folsom and Clovis sites yielded the first indisputable evidence that ancient Americans had co-existed with and hunted the huge, now-extinct mammals called megafauna, including giant bison, mammoths, mastodons, giant ground sloths, and saber-toothed cats. Previously, most scholars had doubted this possibility.

The earliest peoples of the Americas are known as Paleo-Indians. They lived by hunting and gathering. As people began to settle down and expand their diets, they developed what are called Archaic cultures. In addition to foraging, Archaic peoples began to experiment with agriculture.

By about 2300 BC Indians in the Andes Mountains of South America had adopted a fully agricultural way of life. They began to

settle in villages. Farming villages appeared by 2000 BC in Middle America (present-day Mexico and Central America) and somewhat later in Northern America (present-day United States and Canada). Over time these prehistoric farmers developed new kinds of societies. Advanced cultures arose in Middle and South America that rivaled the great civilizations of ancient Egypt, Mesopotamia, and China.

PALEO-INDIANS

The very early people of the Americas were the Paleo-Indians. They shared some cultural traits with peoples of Asia, such as the use of fire and domesticated dogs. However, they do not seem to have used other Old World technologies such as grazing animals, domesticated plants, and the wheel.

Paleo-Indians shared the land with such large mammals as mammoths, mastodons, and giant bison. Archaeological sites of Paleo-Indians often include bones from these animals. This has sometimes led to the mistaken idea that these peoples only hunted big game. By the turn of the 21st century, however, excavations had shown that Paleo-Indians used both animal and wild plant foods, including fruit, tubers, and even seaweed.

American mastodon   woolly mammoth   African savanna elephant

Mastodons and woolly mammoths were hunted by some Paleo-Indians. These animals were similar in size to modern African elephants but, unlike the modern variety, they were adapted to Ice Age temperatures. **Encyclopædia Britannica, Inc.**

CLOVIS AND FOLSOM CULTURES

The best-known Paleo-Indian cultures of North America are Clovis and Folsom. The Clovis culture was the older of the two. Its people left behind one of the most distinctive Paleo-Indian artifact types—the Clovis point. These spear points are leaf-shaped and made of stone. They are also fluted, meaning that they have grooves on each flat side. The culture was named for an archaeological site near Clovis, N.M., where the first such point was found among mammoth bones in 1929. Scrapers (used to clean the hide) and other artifacts used to process meat have also

The Clovis spear point is a characteristic Paleo-Indian artifact. iStockphoto/Thinkstock

been found at Clovis sites. The Clovis culture was long believed to have lasted from about 9500 to 9000 BC. However, early 21st-century research suggested it may have lasted a shorter time, from about 9050 to 8800 BC.

Folsom culture seems to have developed from Clovis culture. It is also known for its own distinctive spear point. Like Clovis points, Folsom points are leaf-shaped, but they are more carefully made and have much larger flutes. The first Folsom point was discovered in 1908 at a site near Folsom, N.M., along with the remains of a now-extinct form of giant bison. The Lindenmeier site, a Folsom campsite in northeastern Colorado, has yielded a variety of scrapers, gravers (used to engrave bone or wood), and bone tools. The Folsom culture is thought to have lasted from about 9000 to 8000 BC. Related Paleo-Indian cultures, such as Plano, continued to between 6000 and 4000 BC.

Pre-Clovis Cultures

Discoveries of several sites in the late 20th century challenged the longstanding belief that Clovis people were the first Americans. Monte Verde, a site in Chile, dates to about 10,500 BC. It is the oldest confirmed site of human habitation in the Americas. A number of other sites may be as early or earlier than Monte Verde. In North America archaeologists have found evidence of pre-Clovis cultures at the Topper site in South Carolina, Cactus Hill in Virginia, and Schaefer and Hebior in Wisconsin.

Archaic Cultures

The Archaic cultures developed from Paleo-Indian traditions. They arose in response to environmental changes. Beginning some 11,500 years ago temperatures rose dramatically worldwide. Large animals such as mammoths could not cope with the change and became extinct. Other animals, such as bison, survived by becoming smaller. At the same time new grasses, trees, and other plants developed.

INNOVATIONS OF THE ARCHAIC INDIANS

As the environment changed, so did the Indians' lifestyles. The most visible change was in their diet. Archaic peoples used a wider range of plant and animal foods than the Paleo-Indians had. They relied more upon smaller animals such as deer and elk.

Bison weathered the escalating temperatures by leading up to the Archaic period becoming smaller. **Ron Levine/The Image Bank/Getty Images**

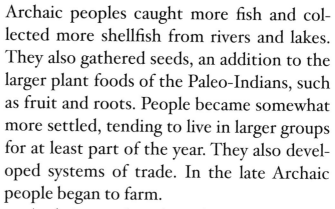

Archaic peoples caught more fish and collected more shellfish from rivers and lakes. They also gathered seeds, an addition to the larger plant foods of the Paleo-Indians, such as fruit and roots. People became somewhat more settled, tending to live in larger groups for at least part of the year. They also developed systems of trade. In the late Archaic people began to farm.

Archaic peoples adapted to their environments by inventing many new technologies. They introduced the spear-thrower, a short, hooked rod that enables a hunter to throw a dart accurately and with great force at a distant target. So-called bird stones may have been used as weights on the spear-thrower to increase the hunter's throwing power. Large fluted points became less popular, replaced by smaller side-notched points more appropriate for hunting with darts. Woodworking tools developed by Archaic peoples included grooved stone axes and gouges made from ground and polished stone.

The spear-thrower was an innovation of the Archaic period. It consisted of a rod with a hook or projection at the rear end to hold the weapon in place until its release. The device gave the spear greater velocity and force. **Encyclopædia Britannica, Inc.**

Two Notable Archaic Cultures

The Cochise culture, an Archaic culture of what is now the southwestern United States, developed techniques for harvesting and processing small seeds. Among their most important tools were milling stones, used for grinding seeds into meal or flour. Later, milling stones were replaced by mortars and pestles. At a later stage of Cochise development, pit houses (houses of poles and earth built over pits) and pottery appeared.

Eastern Archaic people in what are now the U.S. states of Michigan and Wisconsin produced the earliest examples of metalwork in the New World. They cold-hammered pure copper to make tools and weapons. Their Old Copper culture appeared in about 3000 BC and lasted some 2,000 years.

END OF THE ARCHAIC PERIOD

The length of the Archaic period varied across the Americas. It lasted from approximately 8000 BC until at least 2000 BC in most of Northern America, from 7000 to 2000 BC in Middle America, and from 6000 to 2000 BC in South America. But in some places Archaic cultures persisted much longer. For instance, Indians in the Great Basin of the U.S. Southwest kept their foraging lifestyle well into the 1800s.

CHAPTER 2
CIVILIZATIONS OF MIDDLE AMERICA

During the Archaic period the peoples of Middle America made great progress in agriculture. They successfully domesticated squash (about 8000–7000 BC), corn (5000–4000 BC), cassava (5000–4000 BC), and cotton (2600 BC). After obtaining a dependable food supply from agriculture, Middle American peoples settled into villages and had more time to devote to activities such as the arts, architecture, and commerce. Eventually they developed sophisticated civilizations. The great civilizations of Middle America included the Olmec, the Maya, Teotihuacán, the Toltec, and the Aztec.

THE OLMEC

The first great Indian culture in Middle America was that of the Olmec. They lived on the hot, humid lowland coast of the Gulf of Mexico in what is now southern Mexico. San Lorenzo, the oldest known Olmec center, dates to about 1150 BC. At that time the rest of Middle America had only simple farming villages.

The Olmec built large towns where they came together to trade and hold religious ceremonies. The most important were San Lorenzo, La Venta, and Tres Zapotes. They were home to the upper classes of priests and other leaders, who lived in well-made stone houses. These leaders commanded the work of craftsmen and laborers. Farmers lived in the surrounding countryside. Their work

The flat-faced, helmeted "colossal heads" carved by the Olmec people measured up to 9 feet (nearly 3 meters) in height. **Adalberto Rios Szalay — Sexto Sol/Getty Images**

supported the upper classes. Corn was the most important crop.

San Lorenzo is famous for its extraordinary stone monuments. Most striking are the "colossal heads," which are human portraits on a massive scale. They measure up to 9 feet (nearly 3 meters) in height and have flat faces and helmetlike headgear. They may represent players in a sacred rubber-ball game. La Venta is marked by great mounds, a narrow plaza, and several other ceremonial enclosures. Between about 800 and 400 BC it was the most important settlement in Middle America.

The artifacts left by the Olmec range from the huge stone sculptures to small jade carvings and pottery. Much Olmec art depicted a god that is a cross between a jaguar and a human infant, often crying or snarling with open mouth.

The exotic materials used by Olmec artists and craftsmen suggest that the Olmec controlled a large trading network over much of Middle America. Obsidian, a form of volcanic glass used for blades, flakes, and dart points, was imported from highland Mexico and Guatemala. Most imported goods were used to make luxury items. Iron ore, for example, was used to make mirrors.

The Olmec may have developed the first writing system in the Americas. In the late 20th century a stone slab engraved with symbols, or hieroglyphs, that appear to have been Olmec writing was discovered in the village of Cascajal, near San Lorenzo. The Cascajal stone dates to about 900 BC. In the 21st century inscribed carvings similar to later Mayan hieroglyphs were found at La Venta.

Olmec culture began to fade around 400 BC. However, its influence spread north to central Mexico and south to Central America. Among those influenced by the Olmec were the Maya and Teotihuacán civilizations.

THE MAYA

The Maya occupied a nearly continuous territory in southern Mexico, Guatemala, and northern Belize. Before the Spanish conquest of Mexico and Central America, the Maya possessed one of the greatest civilizations of the Western Hemisphere. The rise of the Maya began in about AD 250, and what is known to archaeologists as the Classic Period of Mayan culture lasted until about AD 900. The Maya practiced agriculture, built great stone buildings and pyramid temples, worked gold and copper, and made use of a form of

Mayan ruins at Xunantunich, Belize, c. AD 650–890. © Doug Waugh/
Peter Arnold, Inc.

hieroglyphic writing that has now largely
been deciphered.

AGRICULTURE

As early as 1500 BC the Maya had settled in villages and had developed an agriculture based
on the cultivation of corn, beans, and squash.
By AD 600 cassava was also grown. They practiced mainly slash-and-burn agriculture. First,

The corn god (left) *and the rain god, Chac. Drawing from the Madrid Codex (Codex Tro-Cortesianus), one of the Mayan sacred books.* Courtesy of the Museo de América, Madrid

toward the end of the dry season, a patch of forest was selected for planting. Next, a band of bark would be removed from the trunks of larger trees (the "slash"), which caused the tree to die and shed its leaves. Then the undergrowth and smaller trees were burned and cleared away. The new field was ready to

be planted in time for the first rains. After a few years of planting, the fertility of the soil declined, weeds increased, and the field was abandoned to the forest. The Maya also used advanced techniques of irrigation and, in places with steep land, terracing. Terracing involved leveling off the slopes to make a series of stepped fields.

SETTLEMENTS

By AD 200 the villages and ceremonial centres of the Maya had developed into cities containing temples, pyramids, palaces, courts for playing ball, and plazas. At its height, Mayan civilization consisted of more than 40 cities, each with a population between 5,000 and 50,000. Among the main cities were Tikal, Uaxactún, Copán, Bonampak, Dos Pilas, Calakmul,

Mayan fresco from Bonampak, original c. AD 800, reconstruction by Antonio Tejeda; in Chiapas, Mexico. Ygunza/FPG

Palenque, and Río Bec. The peak Mayan population may have reached 2 million people, most of whom lived in the lowlands of what is now Guatemala.

TECHNOLOGY AND ARTS

To build their cities, the Maya quarried immense quantities of building stone (usually limestone), which they cut using harder stones such as chert. The workers were unaided by

The Temple of Inscriptions, Palenque, Mexico. The Maya considered mountains to be sacred places, and they represented mountains in their cities by building pyramidal stone temples. C. Reyes/Shostal Associates

Jaina pottery figurine, Late Classic Maya style, from Campeche, Mexico; in the collection of Dumbarton Oaks, Washington, D.C. Height 15.5 cm. Courtesy of Dumbarton Oaks, Washington, D.C.

draft animals and wheeled carts, making hauling and construction very labor intensive.

The Maya developed an elaborate and beautiful tradition of sculpture and relief carving. The temples and palaces of Mayan cities were richly ornamented with narrative, ceremonial, and astronomical reliefs and inscriptions that have ensured the stature of Mayan art as premier among American Indian cultures. Architectural works and stone inscriptions and reliefs are also the chief sources of knowledge about the Maya.

SOCIETY

Among the Maya, as in other societies of Middle America, the rulers and nobility were believed to have been created separately from commoners. The result was a highly stratified society in which the work of peasant farmers freed the nobility and the priests from daily drudgery in the fields. The elite used the surplus time to build the cities, pyramids, and temples and to pursue intellectual studies.

Scholars in the mid-20th century mistakenly thought that Mayan society was composed of a peaceful priestly class supported by a devout peasantry. The Maya were believed to be completely absorbed in their religious and cultural pursuits, in favorable contrast to the more warlike peoples of central Mexico. But more recent decipherment of Mayan writing has provided a truer picture of Mayan society and culture. Many hieroglyphs depict the histories of the Mayan dynastic rulers, who waged war on rival Mayan cities and took their aristocrats captive. These captives were then tortured, mutilated, and sacrificed to the gods.

INTELLECTUAL ACHIEVEMENTS

The priestly class was responsible for the impressive development of mathematics and astronomy among the Maya. In mathematics, positional notation and the use of the zero represented a pinnacle of intellectual achievement. Mayan astronomy underlay a complex calendar involving an accurately determined solar year (18 months of 20 days each, plus an unlucky 5-day period), a sacred year of 260 days (13 cycles of 20 named days), and a variety of longer cycles culminating in the Long Count, based on a zero date in 3113 BC. Mayan astronomers compiled precise tables of positions for the Moon and Venus and were able to predict solar eclipses.

One of the great intellectual achievements of Mayan civilization was writing. The Maya developed a system of hieroglyphic writing that they used to record calendars, astronomical tables, dynastic history, taxes, and court records. They made paper from the inner bark of wild fig trees and wrote their hieroglyphs on books made from this paper.

RELIGION

Mayan religion was based on a pantheon of nature gods, including those of the Sun, the Moon, rain, and corn. The priests were responsible for an elaborate cycle of rituals and ceremonies. Torture and human sacrifice were fundamental religious rituals that were thought to guarantee fertility, demonstrate piety, and appease the gods. If such practices

31

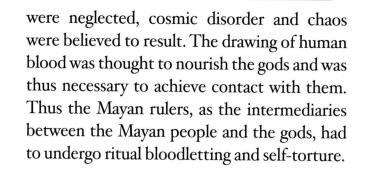

were neglected, cosmic disorder and chaos were believed to result. The drawing of human blood was thought to nourish the gods and was thus necessary to achieve contact with them. Thus the Mayan rulers, as the intermediaries between the Mayan people and the gods, had to undergo ritual bloodletting and self-torture.

Decline

The Classic Maya civilization declined rapidly after AD 900 for reasons that remain uncertain. Some scholars have suggested that armed conflicts and the exhaustion of farmland were responsible, but discoveries in the 21st century led scholars to put forth other explanations. One cause was probably the war-related disruption of river and land trade routes. Other contributors may have been deforestation and drought.

During the Post-Classic Period (900–1519), cities such as Chichén Itzá, Uxmal, and Mayapán in the highlands of the Yucatán Peninsula continued to flourish for several centuries. By the time the Spanish conquered the area in the early 16th century, most of the Maya had become village-dwelling farmers who practiced the religious rites of their ancestors. In the early 21st century more than 5 million people still spoke some 70 Mayan languages.

TEOTIHUACÁN

Located near present-day Mexico City, Teotihuacán was the greatest city of the Americas before the arrival of Europeans. At its height in about AD 500, it covered some 8 square miles (20 square kilometers) and may have housed more than 150,000 people. At the time it was one of the largest cities in the world. It was the region's major economic and religious center.

The origin and language of the residents of Teotihuacán (called Teotihuacanos) are unknown. Perhaps two-thirds of them farmed the surrounding fields. Others made distinctive pottery or worked with obsidian, a form of volcanic glass that was used to make weapons, tools, and ornamentation. The city also had large numbers of merchants, many of whom had emigrated there from great distances. Teotihuacán carried on trade with distant regions, and the products of its craftsmen were spread over much of Middle America. The priest-rulers who governed the city staged grand religious pageants and ceremonies that often involved human sacrifices.

The remains of the ancient city of Teotihuacán in Mexico include pyramids, temples, and palaces. **Gianni Tortoli-Photo Researchers**

The city contained great plazas, temples, palaces of nobles and priests, and some 2,000 single-story apartment compounds. The main buildings were connected by a great street called the Avenue of the Dead. The most prominent feature of Teotihuacán was the Pyramid

34

of the Sun. It dominated the central city from the east side of the Avenue of the Dead. The pyramid is one of the largest structures of its type in the Western Hemisphere, reaching a height of 216 feet (66 meters). The northern end of the Avenue of the Dead was capped by the Pyramid of the Moon and flanked by platforms and lesser pyramids. The second largest structure in the city, the Pyramid of the Moon rose to 140 feet (43 meters).

Near the exact center of the city and just east of the Avenue of the Dead was the Ciudadela ("Citadel"). It was a kind of

The Pyramid of the Moon, the second largest pyramid in Teotihuacán, stands at the northern end of the Avenue of the Dead. Luis Acosta/ AFP/Getty Images

sunken court surrounded on all four sides by platforms supporting temples. In the middle of the sunken plaza stood the Temple of Quetzalcóatl, the Feathered Serpent god. Numerous stone heads of the god projected from the walls of the temple.

In about AD 750, central Teotihuacán burned, possibly during a rebellion or civil war. Although parts of the city were occupied after that event, much of it fell into ruin. Nevertheless, its cultural influence spread throughout Middle America.

THE TOLTEC

The most powerful and culturally advanced civilization in central Mexico from about 900 to 1200 was that of the Toltec people. Toltec culture revolved around the urban center of Tula.

Under the ruler Topiltzin, the Toltec united a number of small states into an empire. Topiltzin introduced the cult of Quetzalcóatl, and he took the name of that god. This cult and others appeared in important Mayan cities to the south in Yucatán, such as Chichén Itzá and Mayapán, and to other Middle American peoples. The Toltec military orders of the Coyote, the Jaguar, and the Eagle also appeared among the Maya. The spread of these cultural traits shows the wide influence of the Toltec.

The exact location of Tula is unknown, but scholars believe it was located near the modern town of Tula, about 50 miles (80 kilometers) north of Mexico City. The town covered at least 3 square miles (some 8 square kilometers) and probably had a population in the tens of thousands. The heart of the town consisted of a large plaza bordered on one side by a five-stepped temple pyramid, which was probably dedicated to Quetzalcóatl. Other structures included a palace complex, two other temple pyramids, and two ball courts. Surrounding Tula were fields watered by irrigation ditches. There the Toltec grew corn, squash, and cotton.

Along with building great palaces and pyramids, the Toltec were known for their metalwork and sculpture. They made fine objects in gold, silver, and copper, which they obtained through an extensive trade network. Their sculptures included the Chac Mools— reclining male figures with a dish resting on the stomach. Thought to represent the rain god Chac, Chac Mools were probably used to hold the hearts of people sacrificed during religious ceremonies.

Beginning in the 1100s the nomadic Chichimec peoples invaded Toltec territory from the north. The invaders destroyed Tula in about 1150 and ended Toltec dominance of central Mexico. Among the Chichimec were the Aztec, who created the next great culture in the region.

THE AZTEC

The dominant group in Middle America when the Spanish arrived was the Aztec. Through conquest, the Aztec had created an empire with a population of 5 to 6 million people. Their language, Náhuatl, spread throughout Middle America as their empire expanded. The capital of the Aztec Empire was Tenochtitlán, on the site of modern-day Mexico City.

AGRICULTURE

The basis of the Aztec's success in creating a great state and ultimately an empire was their remarkable system of agriculture. The Aztec planted a great many crops, of which corn, beans, and squash were the most important. Others included chili peppers, tomatoes, sweet potatoes, cassava, cotton, cacao, pineapples, papayas, peanuts, and avocados. Many crops could be raised only in certain environmental zones, which encouraged trade between regions.

Farming was most intensive in the highlands, where farmers used a variety of special techniques. In places with sloping land, farmers created terraces to control erosion. In some places people built irrigation canals to water their fields. A unique feature of Aztec agriculture was the use of *chinampas*. These artificial islands were built up above the surface of a lake using mud and vegetation from the lake floor. After settling, the *chinampa* was a rich planting bed. Tenochtitlán depended on *chinampas* for much of its food.

In the lowlands, people typically practiced slash-and-burn farming, often supplemented by "raised-field" farming. In the latter method, small earthen hills were built for planting in shallow lakes or marshy areas, similar to the *chinampas* of the highlands. In addition, farmers constructed terraces in some lowland regions.

SETTLEMENTS

With their long history of farming, the Aztec established villages earlier than most

39

TENOCHTITLÁN

The city of Tenochtitlán was founded in about 1325. According to Aztec legend, one of their leader priests, Tenoch, had a vision in which the god Huitzilopochtli instructed the Aztec to look for a sacred site marked by an eagle perched on a cactus and eating a snake. After much wandering, the Aztec found this sign on an island in Lake Texcoco, and there they founded Tenochtitlán. The city's name means "Place of the High Priest Tenoch." The story of the city's foundation is depicted on Mexico's flag and official seal.

In the 1400s Tenochtitlán formed a confederacy with the neighboring states of Texcoco and Tlacopán and became the Aztec capital. Through the construction of *chinampas*, the city gradually expanded into the surrounding lake. It was connected to the mainland by several causeways. Disastrous floods occasionally threatened the city, so its rulers built a series of levees for flood control. They also built aqueducts to supply fresh water and canals to allow canoes to travel throughout the city and to settlements on the lake edges.

The Aztec used their wealth and power to provide a brilliant life in their capital. Montezuma II, the last great Aztec emperor, lived in a splendid palace that was said to consist of 300 rooms. He was surrounded by his nobles and served by thousands of slaves. In the palace grounds were beautiful gardens and menageries. Tenochtitlán also had hundreds of temples.

other Indians. The basic requirement for settlement was water, and the main settlement sites were near major rivers and high valley lakes. Through the years, as their farming skills improved, their settlements grew larger. Some developed into great cities, such as Tenochtitlán.

The type of house in which a person lived was based on wealth and social class. The upper classes lived in two-story palaces of stone, plaster, and concrete. Merchants and the rest of the middle class typically had one-story adobe houses. Each house was built around a patio and raised on a platform for protection against lake floods. Commoners lived in small huts.

TECHNOLOGY AND ARTS

The advanced culture of the Aztec is especially remarkable considering that their technology was quite simple. Their tools were made mostly of chipped and ground stone, and with no large domesticated animals available, all power was based on human energy. In farming, the Aztec used stone axes to clear vegetation and wooden digging tools to work the soil. They ground corn into dough on milling stones called manos and metates.

A notable skill of the Aztec was stone sculpture. The most prevalent sculptures were images of the gods carved for display in temples and public spaces. Aztec woodworkers made large dugout canoes, sculpture, drums, stools, and a great variety of household items. The Aztec also worked metals—gold, copper, and sometimes silver—to produce jewelry and some tools. Their ceramics included pottery, figurines, and musical instruments.

SOCIETY

Aztec society was based on a complex hierarchy. At the top was the ruling class, consisting of priests and nobles. At the bottom were the serfs and slaves. Serfs worked on private and state-owned

Aztec earth goddess Coatlicue. The Aztec were skilled sculptors who often carved images of their gods for public display. DEA/G. Dagli Orti/De Agostini Picture Library/Getty Images

rural estates. Slaves were used mostly for human sacrifice. A man could move up in class through promotions, usually as a reward for valor in war, and women were similarly rewarded for braving the dangers of child-birth. Certain occupations—such as merchants, goldsmiths, and featherworkers—were given more prestige than others.

Trade linked the far parts of the Aztec Empire with Tenochtitlán. Agricultural products, luxury items, and other goods were exchanged at well-organized markets. Soldiers guarded the traders, and troops of porters carried the heavy loads. Canoes brought the crops from nearby farms through the canals to markets in Tenochtitlán. Trade was carried on by barter because the Aztec had not invented money. Change could be made in cacao beans.

INTELLECTUAL ACHIEVEMENTS

The intellectual achievements of the Aztec included the creation of an accurate calendar. It was based on observation of the heavens by the priests, who were also astronomers. The Aztec calendar was common in much of the region. It included a solar year of 365 days and a sacred year of 260 days. An almanac gave dates for fixed and movable religious

festivals and listed the various gods who held sway over each day and hour. The Aztec had hieroglyphics and number symbols with which they recorded religious events and historic annals.

RELIGION

Religion was a powerful force in Aztec life. The Aztec worshipped a host of all-powerful

The Aztec perform a round dance for Quetzalcóatl and Xolotl (a dog-headed god who is Quetzalcóatl's companion). The illustration comes from a reproduction of the Codex Borbonicus, an Aztec manuscript. **Courtesy of the Newberry Library, Chicago**

gods. Some gods personified the forces of nature, such as the sun and the rain. Others were associated with basic human activities, such as war, reproduction, and agriculture. There were also gods of craft groups, social classes, and governments.

To obtain the gods' aid, worshippers performed penances and took part in innumerable elaborate rituals and ceremonies.

An Aztec priest performs a sacrificial offering of a living human heart to the war god Huitzilopochtli. The illustration comes from a reproduction of an Aztec manuscript called the Codex Magliabecchi. Library of Congress, Washington, D.C. (neg. no. LC-USZC4-743)

Each god had one or more special ceremonies, in which offerings and sacrifices were made to gain the god's favor. Human sacrifice played an important part in the rites. Because life was humankind's most precious possession, the Aztec reasoned, it was the most acceptable gift for the gods. As the Aztec Empire grew powerful, more and more sacrifices were needed to keep the favor of the gods. Records indicate that 20,000 captives taken in battle were killed at the dedication of the great pyramid temple in Tenochtitlán. They were led up the steps of the high pyramid to the altar, where chiefs and priests took turns at slitting open their bodies and tearing out their hearts.

SPANISH CONQUEST

The Aztec Empire was at the height of its power when the Spanish arrived in 1519. The ninth emperor, Montezuma II (reigned 1502–20), was taken prisoner by Hernando Cortez and died in custody. His successors, Cuitláhuac and Cuauhtémoc, were unable to stave off Cortez and his forces. With the Spanish capture of Tenochtitlán in 1521, the Aztec Empire came to an end.

CHAPTER 3
CIVILIZATIONS OF SOUTH AMERICA

Civilizations began to develop in the central Andes Mountains of South America by approximately 2300 BC. For several thousand years they became increasingly elaborate, both culturally and technologically. By about AD 1000 these peoples were organized into a number of kingdoms, including Tiwanaku and Chimú. The Inca civilization was formed later and thrived until the Spanish invasion of the early 1500s.

THE TIWANAKU KINGDOM

The main ruins of the kingdom of Tiwanaku are located near the southern shore of Lake Titicaca in what is now Bolivia. Scholars believe that much of the site dates from about AD 200–600, though construction continued until about 1000. During the height of its power, Tiwanaku dominated or influenced large portions of what are now eastern and southern Bolivia, northwestern Argentina, northern Chile, and southern Peru.

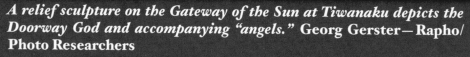

A relief sculpture on the Gateway of the Sun at Tiwanaku depicts the Doorway God and accompanying "angels." **Georg Gerster—Rapho/ Photo Researchers**

Although archaeologists once thought Tiwanaku was mainly a ceremonial site, new finds in the late 20th century revealed that it was a bustling city. Among the main buildings is the Akapana Pyramid, a huge platform mound or stepped pyramid. The Kalasasaya is a low rectangular platform enclosed by alternating tall stone columns and smaller rectangular blocks. A notable feature of the Kalasasaya is the monolithic Gateway of the Sun, which is adorned with the carved central figure of a staff-carrying Doorway God as well as other smaller, winged figures that are sometimes called angels. Another feature of the site is a number of large and finely finished stone blocks with niches, doorways, and recessed geometric decorations. Tiwanaku pottery was painted with black, white, and light red representations of pumas, condors, and other creatures on a dark red background.

The influence of Tiwanaku was largely a result of its remarkable agricultural system. This farming method, known as the raised-field system, consisted of raised planting surfaces separated by small irrigation ditches, or canals. This system was designed in such a way that the canals retained the heat of the intense sunlight during frosty nights and thus kept the crops from freezing.

The Tiwanaku culture vanished by 1200. Scholars have speculated that the present-day Aymara Indians of highland Bolivia are descended from the people of Tiwanaku.

THE CHIMÚ KINGDOM

The Chimú kingdom originated in northern Peru in about AD 1000 and expanded southward, overlapping the northern territory of

The ruins of Chan Chan, Peru, include fascinating examples of adobe mud streets, reservoirs, and walls. Shutterstock.com

Tiwanaku as that kingdom's influence began to decline. Chimú grew into a powerful kingdom in the 1300s and for two centuries reigned as the chief state in Peru.

Chimú was ruled from the city of Chan Chan, on Peru's northern coast. Chan Chan is one of the world's most notable archaeological sites, with 14 square miles (36 square kilometers) of ruins. Among them are rectangular blocks and streets, great walls, reservoirs, and pyramid temples, all built of adobe mud. Chan Chan's population must have numbered many thousands.

Chimú culture was based on farming, which was aided by immense irrigation works. The Chimú seem to have had an elaborate system of social classes ranging from peasants to nobles. They produced fine textiles and gold, silver, and copper objects. They also made pottery in standardized types, which they produced in quantity using molds. The Chimú spoke Yunca (also called Yunga or Moche), a now-extinct language, but had no writing system.

Between 1465 and 1470 the Chimú were conquered by the Inca. The Inca absorbed much from Chimú culture, including their political organization, irrigation systems, and road engineering.

THE INCA

When the Spanish reached Peru in 1532, they encountered the vast empire of the Inca. The great civilization of the Inca extended along the Pacific coast of South America from modern Ecuador southward to central Chile and inland across the Andes. The Inca had conquered this huge territory in a single century, and they ruled its people through a highly organized government. At the peak of

their power the Inca ruled some 12 million people of more than 100 ethnic groups. Most of the people eventually spoke Quechua, the Inca language, at least as a second language.

AGRICULTURE

The Inca civilization flourished because intensive agriculture provided an ample food supply. The Inca achieved this despite harsh growing conditions such as frost on most nights of the year in the highlands. In areas with steeply sloping terrain, they built stone terraces to increase the amount of flat land for crops. Inca farmers raised corn, beans, squash, potatoes, quinoa, sweet potatoes, cassava, peanuts, cotton, peppers, tobacco,

Domesticated alpacas provided the Inca with wool and carried heavy loads. **Allan Baxter/Photographer's Choice RF/Getty Images**

coca, and dozens of other plants. They developed thousands of varieties of their crops to suit different growing conditions. For example, they raised certain kinds of tubers and grains that thrived at high altitudes.

The Inca also domesticated llamas and alpacas. They raised vast herds of these animals to carry loads and to supply wool and sometimes meat. They also raised guinea pigs for meat.

SETTLEMENTS

Inca villages first developed in coastal valleys where water was available for irrigation. Settlements then spread to the high Andean plateau, where some grew into cities. The largest city was Cuzco, the Inca political and religious capital. It had tens of thousands of inhabitants, perhaps as many as 200,000. (By comparison, London, England, had a population of more than 100,000 in 1550.) Most Inca settlements were small villages, however, home to a few hundred people.

The Inca reserved their most remarkable architecture for public buildings. They built massive stone palaces, temples, and fortresses without the use of mortar. Some of the walls still stand. They cut the stones precisely,

fitting them so tightly that not even a knife blade can be inserted into most seams.

The most famous Inca ruins today lie to the northwest of Cuzco at Machu Picchu, perched on steeply sloping land between two sharp peaks. Its numerous white granite structures include temples and other ceremonial sites, palaces, and small houses at various levels connected by stone staircases. Surrounding the residential area are hundreds of well-built stone terraces for farming that were once watered by an aqueduct system.

TECHNOLOGY AND ARTS

The Inca placed a high value on craftsmanship. Their technology differed little from that of surrounding areas, but their products were exceptional for their quality and variety. The most outstanding items were made for the government and the nobility by highly skilled artisans.

Notable crafts of the Inca included metalworking, pottery making, and weaving. In

Machu Picchu ruins. **Linda Whitwam/Dorling Kindersley/Getty Images**

A warrior figure is an example of Inca pottery. iStockphoto/ Thinkstock

addition to gold and silver ornaments, metalworkers made knives, axes, chisels, needles, and other tools from copper and bronze. Potters produced both everyday wares and fine ceremonial pieces for religious uses. Weaving was the most important art. Inca weavers made not only clothing but also colorful textiles and tapestries, often with complicated patterns.

The Inca built an extensive network of roads throughout the empire. The two main royal highways ran north–south, one along the coast and the other across the mountains. Each was about 2,250 miles (3,600 kilometers) long. Many other roads linked the two main highways. The system also included short rock tunnels and suspension bridges supported by woven cables. Only people on official state business were supposed to use the highways.

SOCIETY

Inca society was highly stratified, with people occupying various social ranks by birth. At the top of society was the emperor. Considered a child of the sun, the emperor ruled by divine right and had absolute authority. Below him were all those who were ethnically Inca. These Inca nobles filled all the most important positions in government, the military, and the state religion. Some important posts were filled with people considered to be "Inca by privilege." People granted this status were generally from loyal non-Inca groups of the Cuzco valley. Below them were the various local chiefs and lords. Finally, the bulk of the people were commoners, most of whom made a living by farming or herding animals.

RELIGION

The Inca created a highly organized state religion based on the worship of their sun god, Inti. The Inca believed Inti was their divine ancestor. The Inca also worshipped the Andean god Viracocha, creator of the universe, the other gods, and people and animals.

In the name of their gods, the Inca took control of new lands and spread their religion.

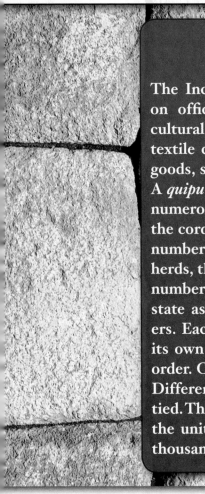

INCA ACCOUNTING

The Inca had no written language, so they relied on official "memorizers" to preserve important cultural information. The Inca also used a type of textile called a *quipu* to keep detailed accounts of goods, services, and people throughout the empire. A *quipu* consisted of a long cord from which hung numerous secondary cords. Officials tied knots in the cords in patterns that tallied such things as the number of llamas in a particular herd or all the state herds, the population of a particular village, and the number of people from each place who served the state as soldiers, road builders, farmers, or weavers. Each commodity or service to be counted had its own cord, probably arranged in a conventional order. Cords were also differentiated by their color. Different types of knots and clusters of knots were tied. The position of the knots on each cord indicated the units they represented—ones, tens, hundreds, thousands, or more.

As they expanded their territory, they incorporated some of the major local gods into the state religion. The Inca allowed the various groups within the empire to continue practicing their own religions, as long as they also worshipped Inti. They also had to farm the land and raise the herds that provided Inti and his priests with food and cloth.

On every important occasion, the Inca made sacrifices to the gods of valued items such as food, *chicha* (a beer made from corn), fine cloth, coca leaves, guinea pigs, and llamas. When a new emperor took office and in times of extreme need—such as great famine, disease, and defeats in battle—the Inca sacrificed humans. The victims were children who were considered physically perfect.

SPANISH CONQUEST

In 1531 Francisco Pizarro, a Spanish adventurer, led an expedition into Inca territory. Finding the empire divided by a recent civil war over the throne, Pizarro captured Atahuallpa, the Inca emperor, in 1532 and had him executed. By 1535 the empire was lost. However, Quechuan-speaking Indians descended from the Inca still remain the dominant native language group in the central Andes.

Francisco Pizarro. Hulton Archive/Getty Images

59

CHAPTER 4

PREHISTORIC FARMING CULTURES OF NORTHERN AMERICA

I n Northern America the transition from an Archaic way of life based mainly on hunting and gathering to one more dependent on agriculture took longer than it did in Middle and South America. Prehistoric farming peoples of Northern America shared certain similarities. They lived more settled lives than Archaic groups, though most still did some hunting away from their settlements. They often protected their communities with walls or ditches. And many farming peoples developed hierarchical societies in which a class of priests or chiefs had authority over one or more classes of commoners.

THE SOUTHWEST

In the first centuries AD three major farming cultures arose in the Southwest: the Ancestral Pueblo (also known as the

In the first centuries AD, three major farming cultures arose in southwestern North America: the Ancestral Pueblo, the Mogollon, and the Hohokam. Each of these cultures reached its height between about AD 700 and 1300.

Prehistoric Farmers of the Southwest

- ■ Major site
- • Modern city
- --- Modern state boundaries
- — Modern international boundaries

UTAH

COLORADO

Denver

NEVADA

ANCESTRAL PUEBLO

UNITED STATES

Las Vegas

Mesa Verde

Durango

Tsegi Canyon

Aztec Ruins

Black Mesa

Salmon Ruin

ARIZONA

Flagstaff

Chaco Canyon

Santa Fe

Colorado R.

Little Colorado R.

Albuquerque

CALIFORNIA

HOHOKAM

Grasshopper

Kinishba

Colorado R.

Gila R.

Phoenix

Point of Pines

Gila Bend

Casa Grande

San Pedro R.

Gila Cliff Dwelling

NEW MEXICO

Tuscon

MOGOLLON

El Paso

TEXAS

Rio Grande

Paquimé (Casas Grandes)

SONORA

CHIHUAHUA

Chihuahua

Guaymas

MEXICO

Gulf of California

PACIFIC OCEAN

SINALOA

DURANGO

0   100   200 mi

0   100   200   300 km

A COMPTON'S MAP

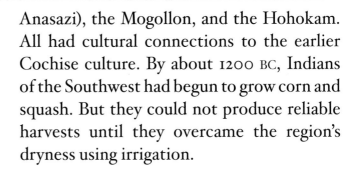

Anasazi), the Mogollon, and the Hohokam. All had cultural connections to the earlier Cochise culture. By about 1200 BC, Indians of the Southwest had begun to grow corn and squash. But they could not produce reliable harvests until they overcame the region's dryness using irrigation.

ANCESTRAL PUEBLO CULTURE

The Ancestral Pueblo lived on the plateau where the U.S. states of Colorado, New Mexico, Arizona, and Utah now meet. Their culture began in about AD 100. At first these people combined hunting, gathering wild plant foods, and some corn cultivation. They typically lived in caves or in shallow pit houses—structures of poles and earth built over underground pits. They also created pits in the ground that were used for food storage.

As farming became more important, the Ancestral Pueblo built irrigation structures such as reservoirs and check dams—low stone walls used to catch runoff from the limited rains. Hunting and gathering became secondary to farming, and the Ancestral Pueblo adopted a more settled lifestyle. Originally, they built partly underground houses in caves or on the tops of high, rocky plateaus

The Cliff Palace, an Ancestral Pueblo dwelling in Mesa Verde National Park in Colorado, has 150 residential rooms and several towers. © C. McIntyre — PhotoLink/Getty Images

called mesas. Later they built above-ground dwellings, both on mesas and in canyons. Using stone masonry they constructed a number of large communities, some with more than 100 adjoining rooms. Kivas—underground circular chambers used mainly for ceremonial purposes—became important community features. Pottery came into widespread use.

CLIFF DWELLINGS

The cliff dwellings built by the Ancestral Pueblo rank among the most striking achievements of prehistoric Native Americans. Set along the sides or under the overhangs of cliffs, these massive structures were much like apartments. They had 20 to as many as 1,000 rooms on multiple stories.

The use of hand-cut stone building blocks and adobe mortar (a wet clay mixture) in cliff dwellings was unmatched even in later buildings. Ceilings were built by laying two or more large crossbeams and placing on them a solid base of smaller branches. The layers were then plastered over with the same adobe mixture used for the walls. Dwellings often consisted of two, three, or even four stories. They had a stepped appearance because each level or floor was set back from the one below it. The roofs of the lower rooms served as terraces for the rooms above.

Residential rooms measured about 10 by 20 feet (3 by 6 meters). Entrance to ground-floor rooms was by ladder through an opening in the ceiling. Rooms on upper floors could be entered both by doorways from adjoining rooms and by openings in the ceiling or roof. Each community had two or more kivas (ceremonial rooms).

Earlier Ancestral Pueblo villages were built in the open. Scholars believe that these people began to build cliff dwellings as a defense against invading groups that may have been the ancestors of the Navajo and Apache. In addition to the natural protection of the cliff, the absence of doors and windows to the rooms on the ground floor left a solid outer stone wall that could be surmounted only by climbing a ladder. The ladders could easily be removed if the town were attacked.

Many smaller communities joined together to form the large towns built beneath the cliffs. Two of the largest, the Cliff Palace at Mesa Verde in Colorado and Pueblo Bonito at Chaco Canyon in New Mexico, probably had about 150 and 800 residential rooms, respectively.

The architecture of the Ancestral Pueblo culminated with the cliff dwellings. Built between 1150 and 1300, these massive houses were set along the sides or under the overhangs of cliffs. Large, apartment-like structures were also built along canyons or mesa walls. The population became concentrated in these large communities, and many smaller villages and hamlets were abandoned. Agriculture continued to be the main economic activity, and craftsmanship in pottery and weaving achieved its finest quality during this period.

The Ancestral Pueblo abandoned their communities by about 1300. A drought lasting from 1276 to 1299 probably caused massive crop failure. At the same time, conflicts increased between the Ancestral Pueblo and neighboring groups that may have been the predecessors of the modern Navajo and Apache peoples. The Ancestral Pueblo moved to the south and the east, near better water sources. The descendants of the Ancestral Pueblo make up the modern Pueblo Indian tribes.

Mogollon Culture

The Mogollon culture existed from about AD 200 to 1450. The homeland of the Mogollon Indians was the mountainous region of what are now southeastern Arizona and southwestern New Mexico. Their territory also extended southward into what are now the Mexican states of Chihuahua and Sonora.

The Mogollon obtained most of their food by hunting and by gathering wild seeds, roots, and nuts. At first they hunted mostly small prey, such as rabbits and lizards, that could be caught in nets or snares. Later they hunted deer and other larger game. Because the Mogollon lived in the mountains, much of their land was not good for growing crops. But they eventually began to grow corn, squash, and beans. They used small dams to pool rainfall and divert streams for watering crops.

At first the Mogollon lived in small villages of pit houses grouped near a large ceremonial structure. Early pit houses were circular with a ceiling made of wood covered with mud. The entrance was through a tunnel. Later pit houses were rectangular and made of stone. Between about 650 and 850 the Mogollon began to build larger pit structures to serve as ceremonial kivas. The appearance of these structures suggests the influence of the Ancestral Pueblo.

By about 1000 the Mogollon began to replace their pit houses with adobe and

Gila Cliff Dwellings National Monument, New Mexico. The Mogollon gradually began to build apartment-style houses that rose up to three stories high. Shutterstock.com

stone apartment-style houses like those of the Ancestral Pueblo. These houses were built at ground level and rose one to three stories high. These villages sometimes contained 40 to 50 rooms arranged around a plaza. Evidence from this period suggests that Ancestral Pueblo and Mogollon peoples lived peacefully in the same villages.

The Mogollon made the first pottery in the Southwest. At first the pottery was simple, made of red or brown clay and undecorated. Over time the Mogollon included designs on the pots and other vessels. They also learned to make and use paints. The Mimbres were a group of Mogollon who were especially well known for their pottery. It was decorated with imaginative black-on-white designs of insects, animals, and birds or with geometric lines.

The Mogollon culture ended for unknown reasons in the 15th century. The people abandoned their villages, perhaps spreading out over the landscape or joining other village groups.

HOHOKAM CULTURE

Between about AD 200 and 1400 the Hohokam people developed an advanced farming culture along the Salt and Gila rivers in southern Arizona. The Hohokam depended on farming for most of their food. They grew corn and eventually beans and squash. They supplemented their food supply by hunting and gathering wild beans and fruits. Another important crop was cotton, which they used to make cloth.

The Hohokam are famous for their complex network of irrigation canals, which was unsurpassed in prehistoric Northern America. The canals, some as long as 10 miles (16 kilometers), rerouted the Gila and Salt rivers to water the fields. They may have been built by cooperating villages. Some of the more than 150 miles (240 kilometers) of

Hohokam irrigation canals were more complex than those of any other prehistoric culture north of Mexico. **Morey Milbradt/Brand X Pictures/Getty Images**

canals in the Salt River valley were renovated and put back into use in the 20th century.

The early Hohokam lived in villages of widely scattered pit houses made of wood, brush, and mud. After about 775 they built large ball courts, similar to those of the Maya of Mexico, and after 975 enclosed some of their villages with walls. After 1150 the Hohokam learned from their Ancestral Pueblo neighbors to construct multistoried community houses with massive walls of adobe. Some houses were built on top of platform mounds.

The Hohokam were active traders. From Mexican peoples they obtained such goods as rubber balls, copper bells, turquoise, obsidian, and macaws, which they kept as house pets. The Hohokam obtained shells from Indians living near the Gulf of California and the Pacific coast. They etched decorations into the surfaces of these shells with acid, becoming the first people in the world to use this artistic technique. Shell jewelry made by the Hohokam was a valuable trade item. They also made baskets and several kinds of pottery.

The Hohokam people abandoned most of their settlements between 1350 and 1450. It is thought that the drought of the late 1200s, combined with a subsequent period of sparse rainfall, contributed to this process. The Pima and the Tohono O'odham (Papago) peoples are modern descendants of the Hohokam.

THE EAST

Over the centuries Archaic Indians east of the Mississippi River had learned to cultivate such plants as sunflowers, squash, and sumpweed. By about 500 BC, the production of these plants had become the basis of the Adena culture. Later came the Hopewell and Mississippian cultures.

ADENA CULTURE

The Adena culture occupied what is now southern Ohio and lasted from about 500 BC to AD 100, though in some areas it may have started as early as 1000 BC. The Adena were mainly hunters and gatherers, but they also did some farming. They seem to have raised sunflowers, squash, and some other food plants, as well as tobacco for ceremonial purposes. The Adena usually lived in villages of cone-shaped houses. The houses were built by setting poles into the ground, connecting them with grass or branches, and covering the structure with mud. Some Adena lived in rock

Prehistoric Farmers of the East

- ■ Adena sites (500 BC–AD 100)
- ■ Hopewell sites (200 BC–AD 500)
- ■ Mississippian sites (AD 700–1500)
- - - - Modern state boundaries
- ——— Modern international boundaries

MICHIGAN
Norton

PENNSYLVANIA

IOWA

INDIANA
OHIO
Newark
Grave Creek Mound

ILLINOIS
Adena
Mound City

UNITED STATES
Miamisburg
Hopewell
Seip
Serpent Mound
WEST VIRGINIA

Cahokia
Angel

MISSOURI
KENTUCKY
VIRGINIA

NORTH CAROLINA
Mound Bottom

ARKANSAS
TENNESSE
Spiro

SOUTH CAROLINA
Etowah

MISSISSIPPI
Ocmulgee

LOUISIANA
Moundville
GEORGIA

ALABAMA
ATLANTIC OCEAN

Emerald Mound
Marksville

FLORIDA

Gulf of Mexico

Crystal River

0   150   300 mi
0 150 300 450 km

A COMPTON'S

shelters. Artifacts from Adena sites include stone tools, simple pottery, and beads, brace-lets, and other ornaments made from shells and copper obtained through trade.

The most distinctive element of Adena culture was mound building. They buried their dead in large earthen mounds, some of which were hundreds of feet long. They also built great earthworks in the shape of animals. These are called effigy mounds. The mounds were built by heaping up basketful after basketful of earth. Some of these large mounds still exist.

Hopewell Culture

The farming culture of the Hopewell Indians lasted from about 200 BC to AD 500, mainly in southern Ohio. Like the Adena, the Hopewell built elaborate earthworks for burial and other purposes.

Hopewell villages lay along rivers and streams. Houses consisted of pole frames

Early North American farmers east of the Mississippi River are known as Eastern Woodland, and later as Mississippian, peoples. The Adena culture lasted from about 500 BC to AD 100, the Hopewell culture from 200 BC to AD 500, and the Mississippian culture from AD 700 to 1500.

covered with bark, animal hides, or woven mats. The people raised corn and possibly beans and squash but still relied upon hunting and fishing and the gathering of wild nuts, fruits, seeds, and roots. Expert artists and craftsmen made carved stone pipes, a variety of pottery, and spear points, knives, axes, and other tools of flint and obsidian. They also made various ceremonial objects out of copper. The Hopewell traded widely. Material from as far away as the Rocky Mountains and the coasts of the Gulf of Mexico and the Atlantic Ocean has been found in Hopewell sites.

Hopewell Culture National Historical Park in south-central Ohio preserves some of the prehistoric burial mounds made by the Hopewell people. © **Hilit Kravitz**

Some Hopewell mounds appear to have been used for defensive purposes, but more often they served as a place to bury the dead. Some formed the bases of temples or other structures. The size of the mounds at many sites—up to about 30 feet (9 meters) high—has led scholars to believe that communities probably worked together to create them. The people likely labored under the direction of a powerful leader.

MISSISSIPPIAN CULTURE

The last great prehistoric culture in what is now the United States was the Mississippian. Beginning in about AD 700 it spread throughout the Southeast and much of the Northeast. The Mississippian culture was based mainly on the production of corn.

The people lived in large towns governed by priest-rulers. Each town had one or more huge, flat-topped mounds that supported temples or the houses of rulers. These mounds often rose to a height of several stories. They were generally set around a plaza that served as the community's ceremonial and social center. The largest Mississippian town was at Cahokia, near present-day St. Louis, Mo. At its peak, it housed 10,000 to

20,000 people. The site originally consisted of about 120 mounds spread over 6 square miles (16 square kilometers), but some of the mounds and other ancient features have been destroyed. Monk's Mound, the largest mound at Cahokia, is about 1,000 feet (300 meters) long, 700 feet (200 meters) wide, and 100 feet (30 meters) high.

Mississippian peoples were united by a common religion focusing on worship of the Sun and a variety of ancestral figures. An organized priesthood conducted elaborate religious rituals and probably also controlled the distribution of surplus food and other goods. Fine craftwork in copper, shell, stone, wood, and clay often displayed religious symbols. The elaborate designs included feathered serpents, winged warriors, spiders, human faces with weeping or falcon eyes, as well as human figures and many geometric motifs. These elements were delicately engraved, embossed, carved, and molded.

Mississippian people in the Southeast were among those who met the first European explorers. Some Mississippian groups, such as the Natchez, have maintained their ethnic identities into the 21st century.

THE PLAINS

Prehistoric farmers of the Great Plains are known as Plains Woodland and then Plains Village peoples. In this region Archaic peoples dominated until about AD 1, when ideas and perhaps people from Eastern Woodland cultures arrived. Between that time and about AD 1000, Indians of Plains Woodland cultures settled in small villages along rivers and streams. They raised corn, beans, and eventually sunflowers, gourds, squash, and tobacco.

Around AD 1000 Plains peoples began to combine their small villages to form larger settlements. The riverbanks became more densely settled. Thus began the Plains Village period, which lasted until about 1450. Like the Mississippian peoples, these cultures developed elaborate rituals and religious practices. The descendants of the Plains Village groups include such tribes as the Arikara, Mandan, Hidatsa, Crow, and Pawnee.

CONCLUSION

When one thinks of ancient civilizations, those of the Old World—Egypt, Mesopotamia, China, India, Greece, Rome—are typically the first to come to mind. Those of the Americas are sometimes overlooked. However, in the organization of their kingdoms and empires, the sophistication of their monuments and cities, and the extent of their intellectual accomplishments, the civilizations of Middle and South America constitute a New World counterpart to those of the Old World.

Yet the legacies of the Old and New World civilizations are different. While Old World civilizations generally provided the basis for continuing cultural developments, the cultures of the New World were submerged by the Spanish conquerors of the 16th century. Nevertheless, elements of the ancient cultures persist. Visitors to the Mayan cities of the Yucatán, the Inca ruins at Machu Picchu, or the Ancestral Pueblo cliff dwellings of Mesa Verde can hear the echoes of their ancient inhabitants. And the ongoing prevalence of Mayan and Quechuan languages in Middle and South America is a living legacy of the Americas' distant past.

adobe A heavy clay used in making sun-dried bricks ; also refers to the bricks themselves.

annals Historical records.

bloodletting The act or practice of shedding blood.

chert A rock resembling flint.

chicha A South American and Central American beer made chiefly from fermented corn.

chinampa An artificial agricultural island reclaimed from a lake or pond by piling rich soil dredged from the bottom.

featherworker One who uses overlapping ornamental feathers to create clothing, blankets, or other decorative items.

fluted Having or marked by grooves.

irrigation The watering of land by artificial means to foster plant growth.

kiva A Pueblo Indian ceremonial structure that is usually round and partly underground.

mano A stone used as the upper millstone for grinding foods (as Indian corn) by hand in a metate.

mesa An isolated, relatively flat-topped natural elevation usually more extensive than a butte and less extensive than a plateau.

metate A stone with a concave upper surface used as the lower millstone for grinding grains and especially Indian corn.

monolithic Huge; massive.

mortar and pestle A sturdy vessel (mortar) in which material is pounded or rubbed with a usually club-shaped implement (pestle).

pit house An early dwelling structure of poles and earth built over a pit dug in the ground.

porter A person who carries burdens or cargo.

quipu A device made of a main cord with smaller varicolored cords attached and knotted and used by the ancient Inca in accounting.

tuber A short, fleshy, usually underground stem; examples include potatoes and taro.

Archaeological Institute of America
   (AIA)
656 Beacon Street, 6th Floor
Boston, MA 02215-2006
(617) 353-9361
Web site: http://www.archaeological.org
The AIA promotes public interest in the
   cultures and civilizations of the past,
   supports archaeological research, fos-
   ters the sound professional practice of
   archaeology, advocates the preservation
   of the world's archaeological heritage,
   and represents the discipline in the
   wider world.

Foundation for the Advancement of
Mesoamerican Studies, Inc. (FAMSI)
268 South Suncoast Boulevard
Crystal River, FL 34429
(352) 795-5990
Web site: http://www.famsi.org
FAMSI supports research related to
   Mesoamerican cultures by providing
   funding and resources to scholars work-
   ing in related fields. Translations of
   various Mesoamerican writings, maps,
   and other resources for teachers and
   students are also available.

Institute of Maya Studies (IMS)
Miami Science Museum
3280 South Miami Avenue
Miami, FL 33129
(305) 235-1192
Web site: http://www.instituteofmayastudies
.org
The IMS seeks to educate the public on
Mayan civilization as well as aspects of
other pre-Columbian cultures. Its lecture
series features specialists in the field.

Middle American Research Institute (MARI)
Tulane University
6823 St. Charles Avenue
New Orleans, LA 70118
(504) 865-5110
Web site: http://www.tulane.edu/~mari
MARI supports research and spon-
sors projects related to the study of
Mesoamerican cultures and civilizations. A variety of art and artifacts are
on display, and much of the collection
is available to students and faculty for
research purposes.

Museum of Anthropology (MOA)
University of British Columbia
6393 N.W. Marine Drive

Vancouver, BC V6T 1Z2
Canada
(604) 822-5087
Web site: http://www.moa.ubc.ca
The extensive collection of this museum
    includes artifacts from the cultures of
    Mesoamerica that are available to view
    online.

Museum of Archaeology and Ethnology
Simon Fraser University
8888 University Drive
Burnaby, BC V5A 1S6
Canada
(778) 782-3325
Web site: http://www.sfu.museum
The Latin American collections at the
    Museum of Archaeology and Ethnology
    showcase a variety of artifacts from the
    ancient cultures of the region. Resources
    for educators and students are also
    available.

National Museum of the American Indian
    (NMAI)
Fourth Street and Independence Avenue SW
Washington, DC 20560
(202) 633-1000
Web site: http://www.nmai.si.edu

The NMAI has a vast collection of Native American art and artifacts representing more than 1,200 cultures indigenous to the Americas over a period of 12,000 years. Online exhibitions are also available for viewing.

WEB SITES

Due to the changing nature of Internet links, Rosen Educational Services has developed an online list of Web sites related to the subject of this book. This site is updated regularly. Please use this link to access the list:

http://www.rosenlinks.com/ancv/amer

Bancroft-Hunt, Norman. *Historical Atlas of Ancient America* (Mercury, 2009).

Coe, M.D., and Koontz, Rex. *Mexico: From the Olmecs to the Aztecs*, 6th ed., rev. and expanded (Thames & Hudson, 2008).

Foster, L.V. *Handbook to Life in the Ancient Maya World* (Oxford Univ. Press, 2005).

Ganeri, Anita. *Mesoamerican Myth: A Treasury of Central American Legends, Art, and History* (Chartwell, 2007).

Green, Jen, and others. *The Encyclopedia of the Ancient Americas* (Southwater, 2001).

Montgomery, John. *How to Read Maya Hieroglyphs* (Hippocrene, 2003).

Noble, D.G. *Ancient Ruins of the Southwest: An Archaeological Guide*, 2nd ed. (Northland, 2000).

Pauketat, Timothy, and Bernard, N.S. *Cahokia Mounds* (Oxford Univ. Press, 2004).

Phillips, Charles. *Aztec & Maya: The Complete Illustrated History* (Metro, 2008).

Silverman, Helaine, and Isbell, W.H., eds. *Handbook of South American Archaeology* (Springer, 2008).

VanDerwarker, A.M. *Farming, Hunting, and Fishing in the Olmec World* (Univ. of Texas Press, 2006).

Wood, Marion. *Ancient Maya and Aztec Civilizations*, 3rd ed. (Chelsea House, 2007).